BUTTERFLY BEAUTIES

~ A Journal of Hope & Healing ~

My personal journey has been one of struggle
& sometimes pain... of growth & change... of vulnerability...
and at times I was frozen with fear.
In spite of it all ...
I am learning to love myself more each day.

Whatever your journey may be, know this...
"Never Hide Your WINGS"

Please join me on this journey as you colour,
create & connect with your Heart.

Love & light,
JENNIFER ♡

Copyright © 2018
Self-Care Colouring Journals by Jennifer E. Robinson
All rights reserved

No part of this book may be reproduced, transmitted, shared or stored in any form or by any means except for your own personal use, without the express written permission of the author/artist:

WWW.BUTTERFLYBEAUTIES.CO

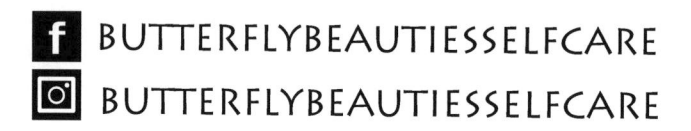

f BUTTERFLYBEAUTIESSELFCARE
◉ BUTTERFLYBEAUTIESSELFCARE

"DOWNLOAD YOUR FREE SELF-LOVE GUIDE @ BUTTERFLYBEAUTIES.CO"

A special Thank you to Steve... for your unwavering love ♡ and support through all my tears, fears and sleepless nights.

BUTTERFLY BEAUTIES

~ A Journal of Hope & Healing ~

JENNIFER E. ROBINSON

For the best
Mindful Colouring
& Journaling Experience...
Pencil Crayons
& Gel Pens
are recommended for
this paperstock.

THE BENEFITS OF COLOURING

1. The action of colouring requires focus which is regulated by the frontal lobe of the brain... the area responsible for executive functioning & self-regulation. When these functions are compromised individuals can experience:
~ difficulty with problem solving
~ impaired judgement
~ trouble focusing

2. Colouring helps you to focus & calm your brain... which leads to health benefits for your mental health.

3. It reduces anxiety, by concentrating on the task in front of you & helps you to achieve an enhanced focus as you aren't thinking about your worries.

4. Colouring stimulates the right side of your brain where our creativity, intuition & visualization lies.

5. It's a great way to detach from our screens that have taken over our lives.

6. Colouring can help you to fall asleep if done right before your bedtime.

TOP REASONS TO JOURNAL

1. It's a Memory Keeper

2. It is one of the best tools to figure out who you are.

3. Journaling helps with healing anxiety & depression from past negative experiences.

4. It is a very healthy & safe way to get out your emotions.

5. It can help increase your expressive writing ability.

6. Journaling is a sacred private space for you alone.

7. It helps you build routine & self-discipline to show up for yourself.

8. Journaling is great for connecting with your passions, dreams & intuition.

9. It is one of the best self-care & self-love practices to get to know yourself without judgement.

10. Journaling is a great creative booster.

This Book belongs to...

_____

Life Lessons from a Butterfly...

Embrace change

Unfurl your wings

Come out of your cocoon

Stop and smell the flowers

Let your beauty show

Never hide your WINGS

LEARNING TO LOVE HER

She is resilient and strong
In spite of the torment and pain
I've starved her and berated her
And locked her in a place of shame

She has fought battles of depression
And earned scars from numerous births
And even then when she produced the miracle of life
A glance in the mirror caused my lips to purse

She has been poisoned with toxins
In hopes of a sleeker design
While I threw words of hatred and anger
Such a harsh punishment for not committing any crime

She's battled abuse, anxiety and judgement
While standing through all the fear
And I shake my head in amazement
Wondering how she is still here

This body of mine is amazing
She should be on a pedestal, wearing a crown
For years she's been treated so badly
Yet she's never let me down

It's time to stop the pain
The self hatred, the harsh words
She has given me years of loyalty
Despite everything she's endured

I've got a lot of wounds to bandage
For every battle she's been through
But it's time to love her and myself
For in life, it's what we're meant to do

~ Jennifer E. Robinson ~

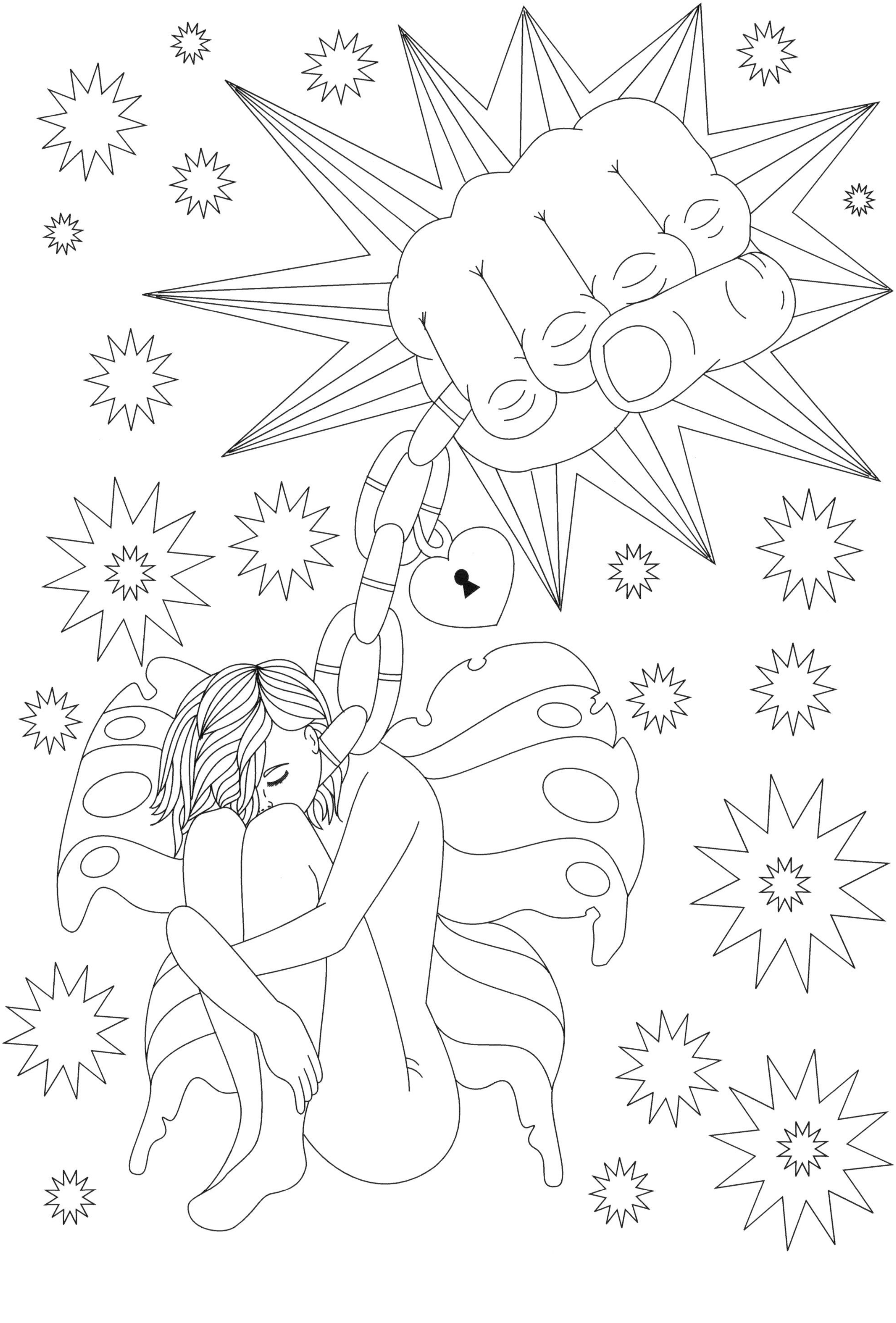

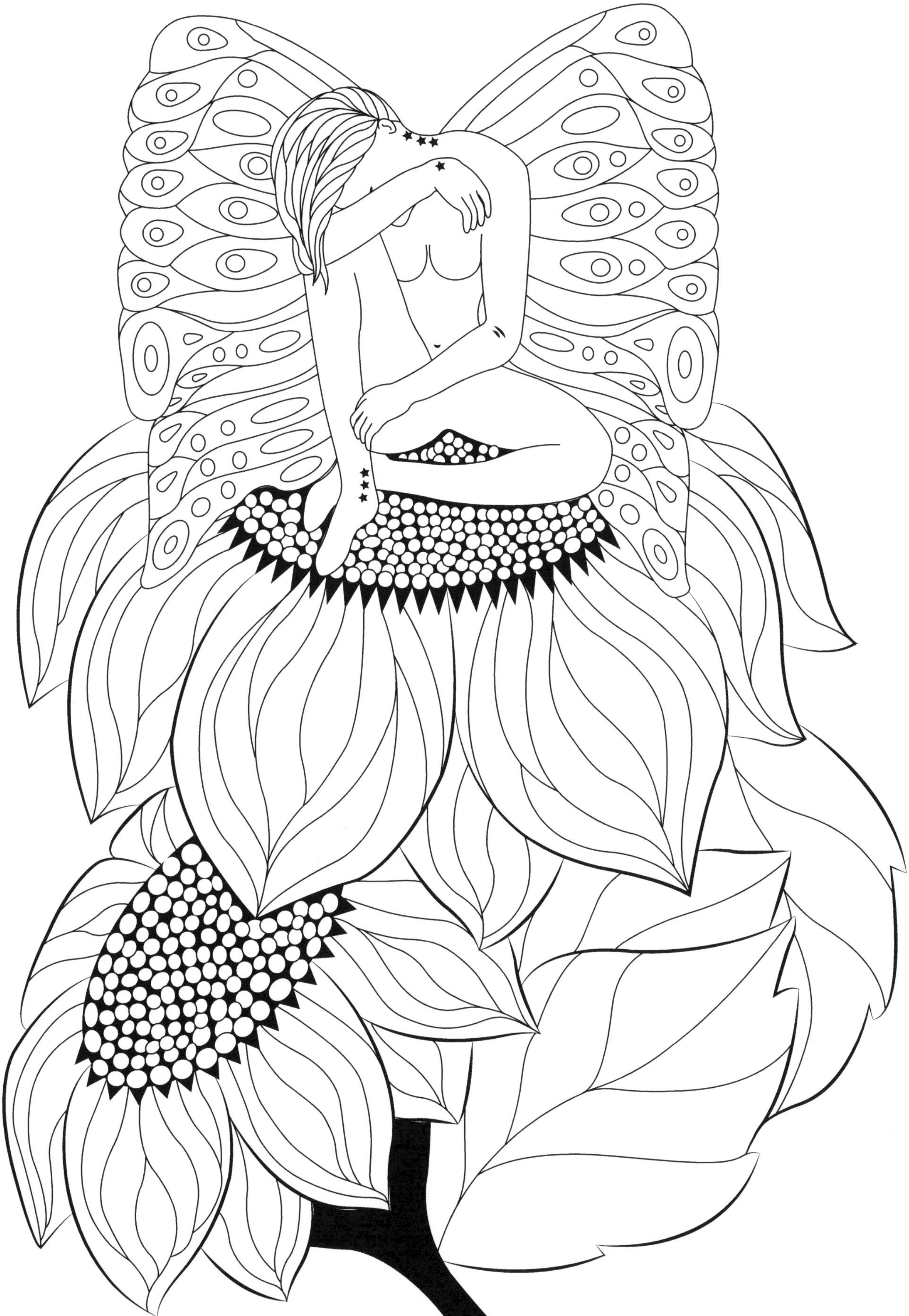

"Perhaps the **Butterfly** is proof that you can go through a great deal of darkness, yet become something **Beautiful**"

~ Beau Taplin ~

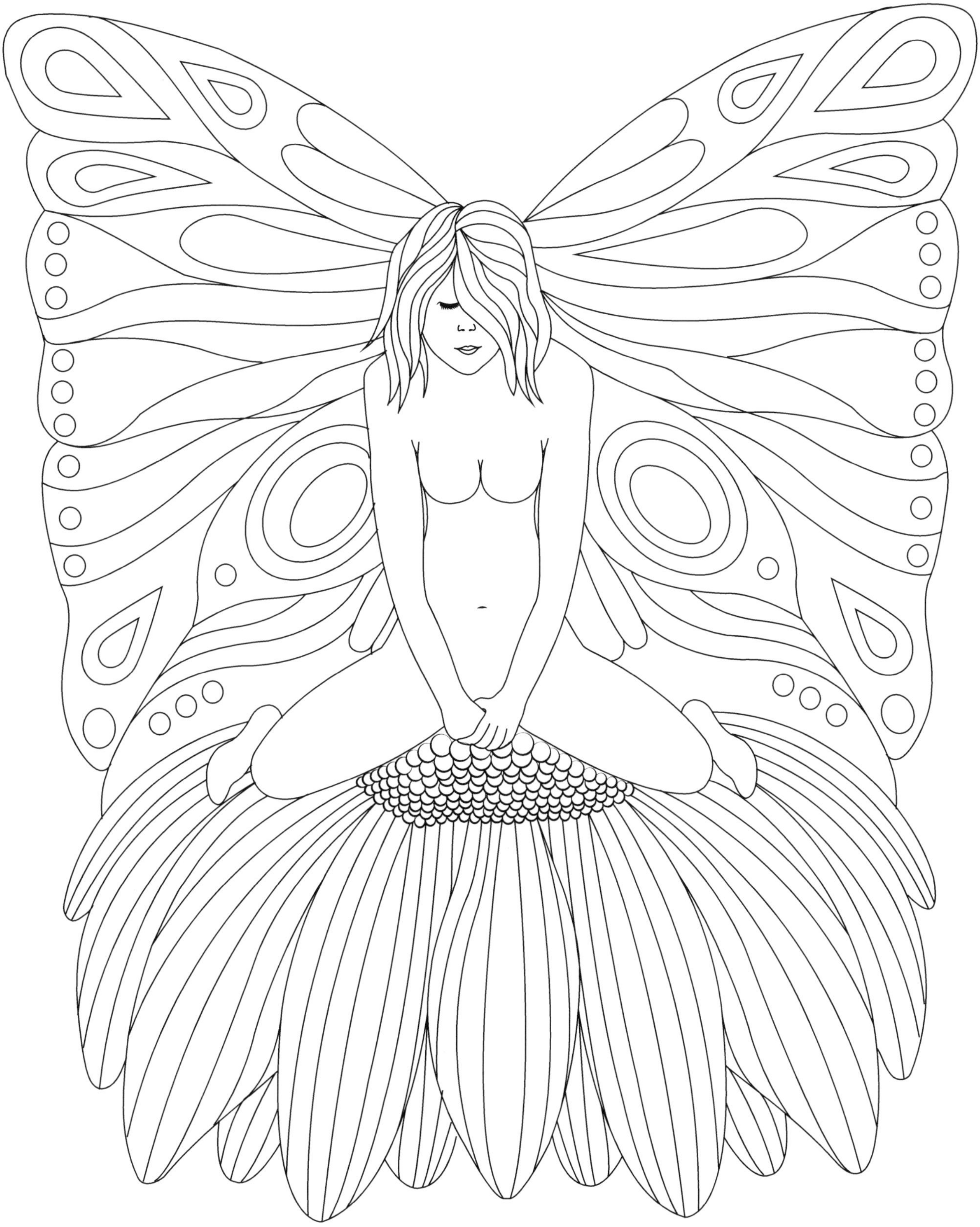

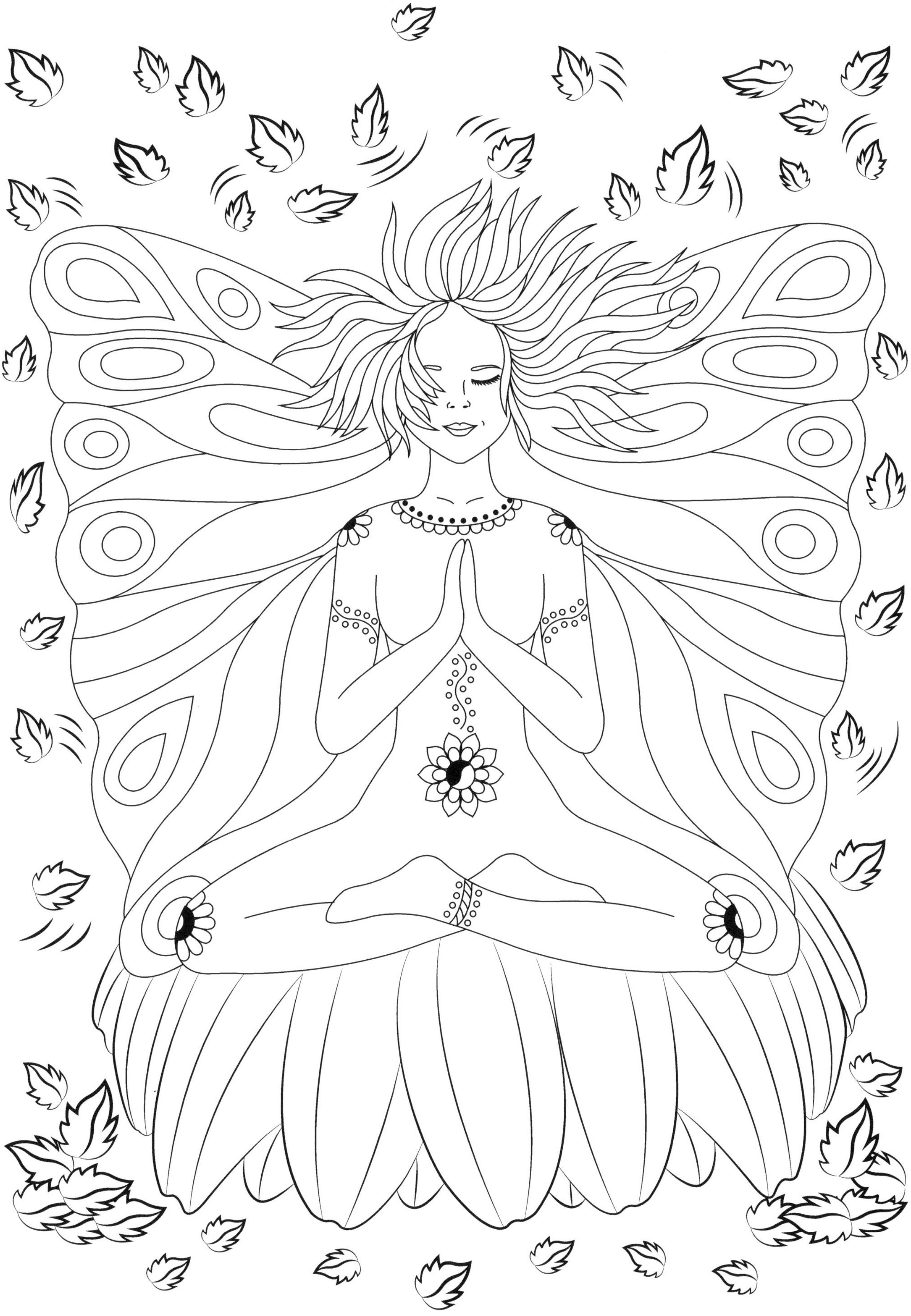

I AM WORTHY OF LOVE

I AM WORTHY OF HEALING

SELF CARE WHEEL

PSYCHOLOGICAL
Support Groups
Journaling, Releasing tears
Accepting your emotions
Reflection, Relaxation
Asking for help

PHYSICAL
Get enough sleep
Eat healthy, Move your body
Express & accept affection, Kiss, Hug
Massages, Bubble Baths
Regular medical care

EMOTIONAL
Laugh, Cry, Hug, Express
Self Love & Acceptance
Take a bath, Treat yourself
Watch a funny movie
Affirmations

LIFE BALANCE

PROFESSIONAL
Leave work at work
Take time for lunch
Set boundaries about overtime
Plan next career moves
Learn to say No

PERSONAL
Foster friendships
Make a Vision Board
Read a book, write a poem
Spend time with loved ones
Explore what you want in life

SPIRITUAL
Meditate, Sit in quiet
Listen to your hearts desires
Spend time in nature
Yoga, Prayer, Relection
Practice self forgivenesss

MY SELF CARE PLAN

I can exercise my body by...

I can be a good friend by...

People I can reach out to...

I can relax my mind & body by...

ME

I can make myself happy by...

New things I'd like to try...

My hopes and dreams...

Healthy foods I eat...

MY SELF CARE PLAN

We all have bad days but what matters is how we deal with those difficult times. Will you let yourself spiral deeper into sadness, or will you pick yourself back up again?

This worksheet is to help you on your darkest days. Answer the questions below and when you are starting to have a down day... come back to this sheet, reread your answers to lift your spirits and remind yourself of your strength and inner beauty.

1. List 10 things you are grateful for:

   _____   _____
   _____   _____
   _____   _____
   _____   _____
   _____   _____

2. What is your favourite thing to do? (with friends, family or on your own time)

   _____
   _____
   _____

3. What is the best compliment that you have ever received?

   _____
   _____

4. Describe your perfect day (the sky is the limit... use your imagination)

   _____
   _____
   _____
   _____

5. What is your favourite flavour of ice cream? _____

Now text or call a friend... tell them you're having a lousy day and that you'd like some company while you treat them to their favourite ice cream flavour.

Mood Tracker

Choose a colour for each mood and track your moods throughout the month.

Use your mood tracker as a tool to reflect on your feelings each month so you can see where you may need to focus on and seek help if needed.

Month:

- [ ] Happy, joyful, relaxed, silly, content, great
- [ ] Productive, active, energetic, motivated
- [ ] Good, average, normal, uneventful
- [ ] Sad, lonely, numb, depressed, insecure
- [ ] Angry, frustrated, anxious, grumpy
- [ ] Sick, tired, lazy, dull, unmotivated, bored

How do I feel at the moment?

What do I need more of in my life?

What is going right in my life?

What am I grateful for?

What makes me come alive?
When was the last time I felt truly alive?

What advice would I give to my younger self?

What drains my energy? How can I reduce it or cut it?

What is something I've always wanted to do but was scared?

1. Place your hand on your heart, close your eyes & breathe slowly for 1 minute.
2. Write out the Affirmations below... over & over until you've filled the lines.

I am worthy of love. I am worthy of Healing.

I am perfect, just as I am.

1. Place your hand on your heart, close your eyes & breathe slowly for 1 minute.
2. Write out the Affirmations below... over & over until you've filled the lines.

I deeply love and accept myself.

I am courageous and I stand up for myself.

I HAVE THE POWER

TO CHANGE MY STORY

INNER CHILD OF MINE

Hello my lovely
Where have you been?
It's been such a long time
Happy to see you again

I tucked you away
All those many years ago
I'm sorry that I left you
It's not my fault, I didn't know

You were just a wee child
So innocent and free
But the world got their claws in you
You were smothered, unable to see

I've missed you so much
I didn't know you were gone
The world bumped and bruised you
It's no wonder you had fallen

Now I promise to love you
For I'm finding my way
I was supposed to protect you
And keep harm at bay

But as I raise my vibration
And find my lost soul
I'll always choose you first
So you can find your way home

I've got a lot of work to do now
But I promise you this
I will always keep you safe inside
So we can live in our highest Bliss

~ Jennifer E. Robinson ~

Open your wings Darling
and spread them out wide,
for the light
that's within you...
is the gift you hold inside.

~ Jennifer E. Robinson ~

> We have to shed the old
> Before we can come into the new

Just a sparkle,
A wee glimmer.
A tiny twinkle is what I see.
I hear her stirrings,
Her stifled whimpers...
She desperately wants
to be Free.

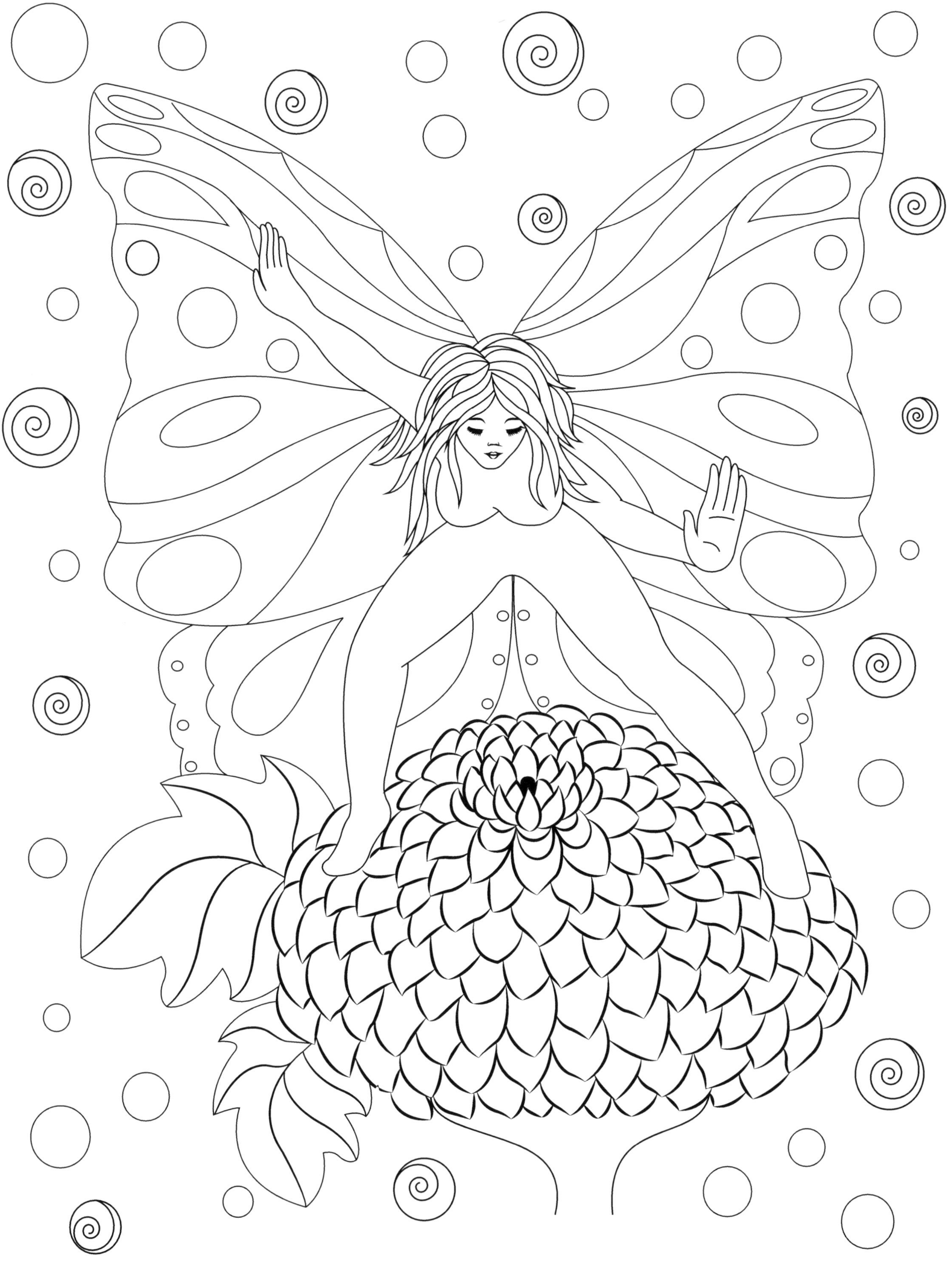

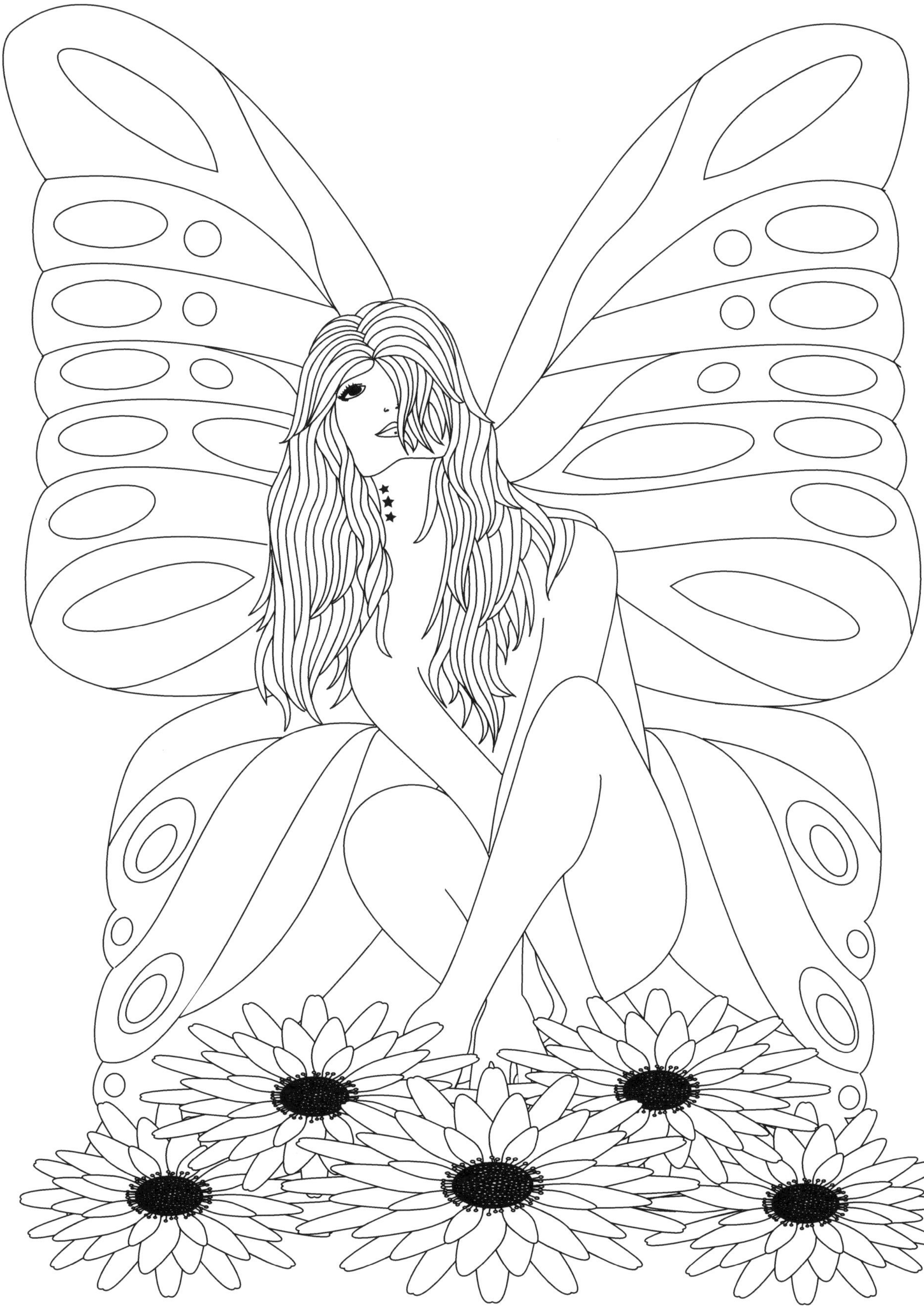

I AM COURAGEOUS

AND I STAND UP FOR MYSELF

10 Steps to a Positive Body Image

1. Remind yourself that "true beauty" is a state of your mind, not your body.

2. Appreciate all that your body can do - each "in" and "out" breath is a miracle of life.

3. Write a top-5 list of things you like about yourself... things that aren't related to your weight or what you look like.

_____
_____
_____
_____
_____

4. Wear clothes that are comfortable and make you feel good about your body.

5. Become a realistic viewer of social media posts and question things..

"Does that image look realistic or attainable? Could it have been photoshopped? Do my friends and family represent those bodies I see on social media? Could there be more behind that person's story that isn't being shown on their social media?

6. Surround yourself with positive people.

7. Look at yourself as a whole person... choose not to focus on specific body parts.

8. Give back to society, help out a friend or do a random act of kindness for someone. Focusing on others will help take the focus off of worrying about food, calories and your weight. It will lift your spirits and put things into perspective. When you give back to others, in essence you are giving back to yourself.

9. Honour your body and do something nice for yourself ~ a bubble bath, pedicure...

10. Practice daily "Positive Body Image" Affirmations ~ "I love & accept myself."

5 THINGS THAT MAKE ME BEAUTIFUL

List some ways that you are beautiful, either on the inside or the outside.

_____

_____

_____

_____

_____

you are so enough, you have no idea how enough you are

Mood Tracker

Choose a colour for each mood and track your moods throughout the month.

Use your mood tracker as a tool to reflect on your feelings each month so you can see where you may need to focus on and seek help if needed.

I AM ENOUGH

Month: _____

- ☐ Happy, joyful, relaxed, silly, content, great
- ☐ Productive, active, energetic, motivated
- ☐ Good, average, normal, uneventful
- ☐ Sad, lonely, numb, depressed, insecure
- ☐ Angry, frustrated, anxious, grumpy
- ☐ Sick, tired, lazy, dull, unmotivated, bored

What are some things that I judge about myself?

What can I do to take better care of myself?

What are 3 actions that I can take to move me towards a more fulfilling life?

What do I like about myself? What do I love about myself?

What/Who inspires me the most? Why am I drawn to those inspirations?

What would make me happy right now?

What does my perfect day look like?

What is something I would love to learn?

1. Place your hand on your heart, close your eyes & breathe slowly for 1 minute.
2. Write out the Affirmations below... over & over until you've filled the lines.

My strength is greater than any struggle.

Each step is taking me to where I want to be.

1. Place your hand on your heart, close your eyes & breathe slowly for 1 minute.
2. Write out the Affirmations below... over & over until you've filled the lines.

I know who I am, and I am enough.

_____
_____
_____
_____
_____
_____
_____
_____
_____

Today, I will not stress over things I can't control.

_____
_____
_____
_____
_____
_____
_____
_____
_____

MY STRENGTH IS GREATER

THAN ANY STRUGGLE

OPEN YOUR WINGS

Open your wings Darling
And spread them out wide
For the light that's within you
Is the gift you hold deep inside

Just a sparkle
A wee glimmer
A tiny twinkle is what I see

I hear her stirrings
Her stifled whimpers
She desperately wants to be free

Unfurl your wings Darling
I know you're scared... I've been there too
But the gift you will experience
Is the power I see in you

~ Jennifer E. Robinson ~

Be your own kind of BEAUTIFUL

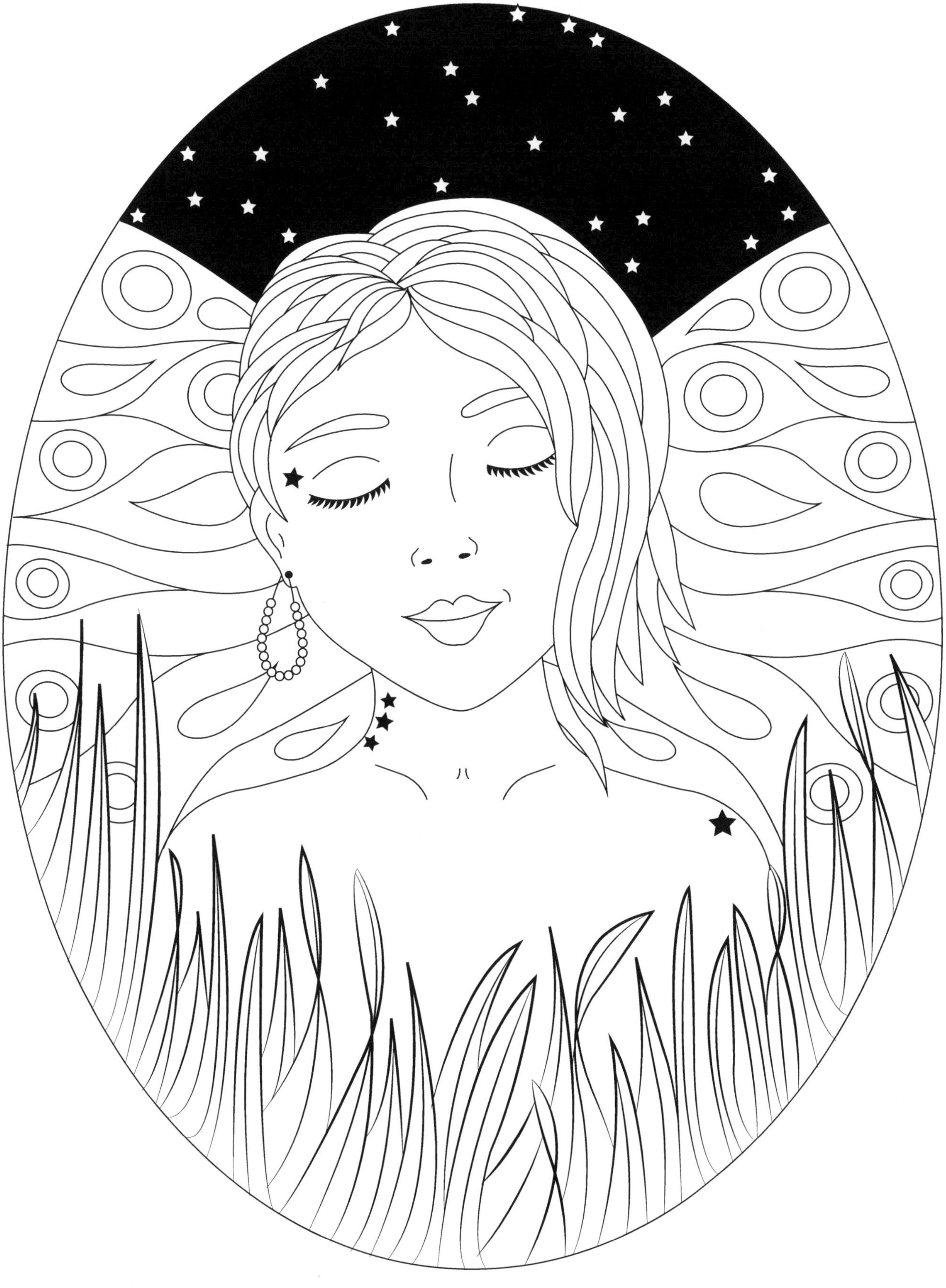

Unfurl your Wings
Darling,
I know you're scared...
I've been there too.
But the Gift you'll
Receive,
Is the POWER
I see in
You!

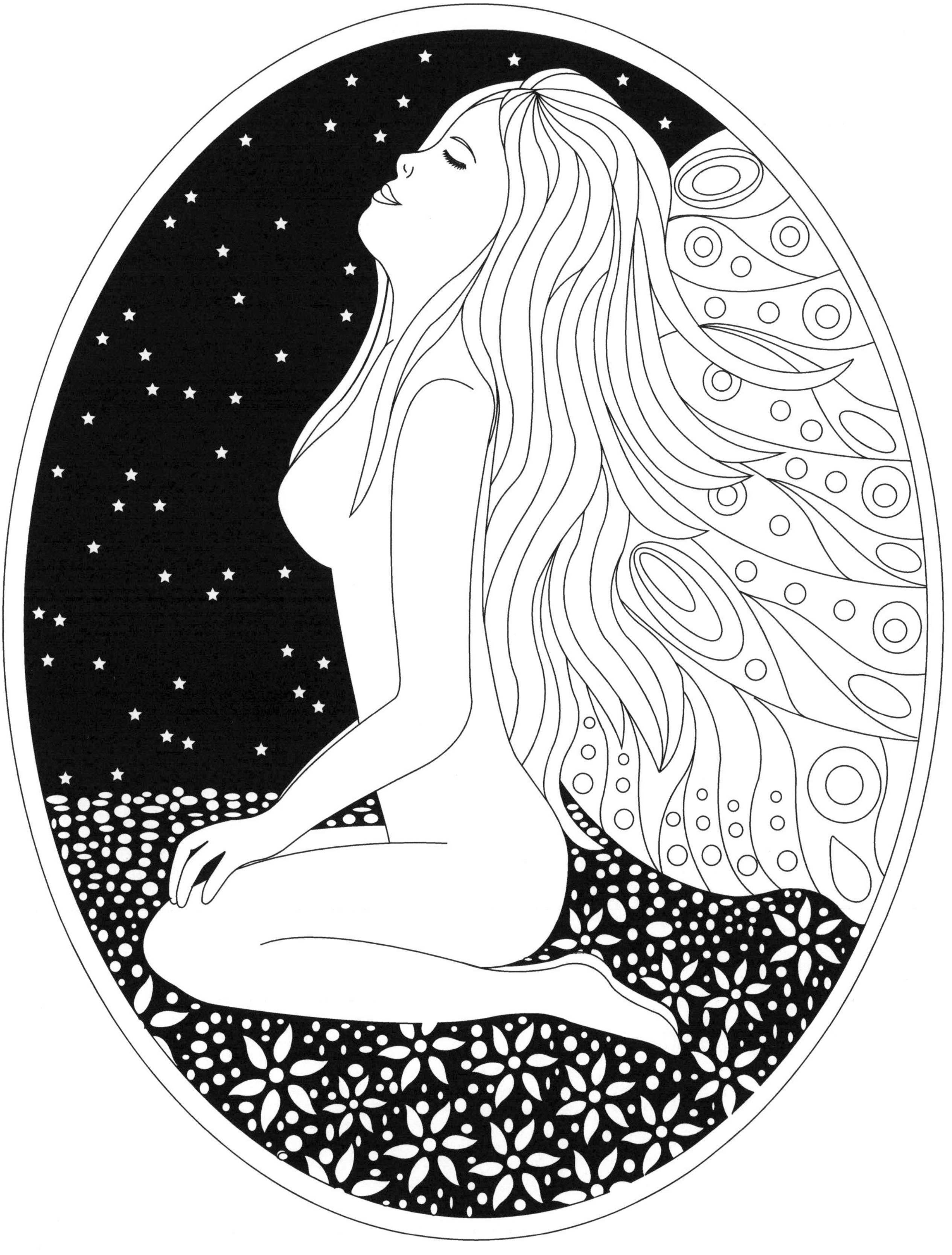

Free to Be Me

I DEEPLY LOVE

AND ACCEPT MYSELF

I HAVE A GROWTH MINDSET

- I like to challenge myself
- Mistakes help me learn
- I can learn anything I want to
- I can always try again & improve
- I'm inspired by people who succeed
- My effort & attitude make a difference

POSITIVE TRAITS LIST

You are encouraged to circle your own positive traits to begin building your self esteem and an awareness of how unique and amazing you are.

There is only one YOU in this world!

Trusting	Empathetic	Hardworking
Brave	Independent	Optimistic
Positive	Open-Minded	Relaxed
Reliable	Innovative	Cooperative
Strong	Respectful	Mature
Focused	Tolerant	Motivated
Creative	Friendly	Forgiving
Confident	Helpful	Realistic
Grateful	Kind	Insightful
Responsible	Selfless	Generous
Loyal	Flexible	Self-Directed
Cheerful	Enthusiastic	Open-Hearted
Nurturing	Funny	Carefree
Thoughtful	Modest	Resilient
Determined	Sensitive	Listener
Patient	Courteous	Beautiful
Accepting	Intelligent	Skilled
Practical	Decisive	Soulful
Frugal	Organized	Loving
Honest	Humble	Huggable

Mood Tracker

Choose a colour for each mood and track your moods throughout the month.

Use your mood tracker as a tool to reflect on your feelings each month so you can see where you may need to focus on and seek help if needed.

Month:

- ☐ Happy, joyful, relaxed, silly, content, great
- ☐ Productive, active, energetic, motivated
- ☐ Good, average, normal, uneventful
- ☐ Sad, lonely, numb, depressed, insecure
- ☐ Angry, frustrated, anxious, grumpy
- ☐ Sick, tired, lazy, dull, unmotivated, bored

What might trigger me today?
What can I do to prepare for the day?

Where does my pain originate?
What would need to happen for me to heal?

What are my small Victories & Successes?

If I had all the time in the world, what would I want to do first?

What lessons did I learn this month?

What are my strengths?   What am I good at?

What are my priorities at the moment?

If I could share one message with the world what would it be?

1. Place your hand on your heart, close your eyes & breathe slowly for 1 minute.
2. Write out the Affirmations below... over & over until you've filled the lines.

I am strong, I am beautiful, I am worthy.

_____
_____
_____
_____
_____
_____
_____
_____
_____

I am following my dreams, so my children will follow theirs.

_____
_____
_____
_____
_____
_____
_____
_____
_____

1. Place your hand on your heart, close your eyes & breathe slowly for 1 minute.
2. Write out the Affirmations below... over & over until you've filled the lines.

I set myself free, by choosing to forgive.

I give myself permission to heal.

I AM GETTING STRONGER

I AM BRAVER THAN I THINK

ALL THAT I AM

My knees quiver, my body shakes
I desperately want to be free
I lift my heart up to the sky
I'm on a journey of finding me

I am scared but I won't falter
It's going to be different this time
I have the power to change my story
I am worthy of love... this beautiful life will finally be mine

I deeply love and accept myself
I am perfect just the way I am
My strength is greater than any struggle
This time I'll make it, because I have faith and I have a plan

I am worthy of love, I am worthy of healing
I'm ready to fly and let my spirit soar
I am courageous... I stand up for all that I am
Look out world, I'm coming ... Hear me Roar!

~ Jennifer E. Robinson ~

Follow your Dreams

Just Breathe

Spread out your
Wings,
And reach for the sky.
Your Brave Heart
awaits you...
She is eager to
FLY

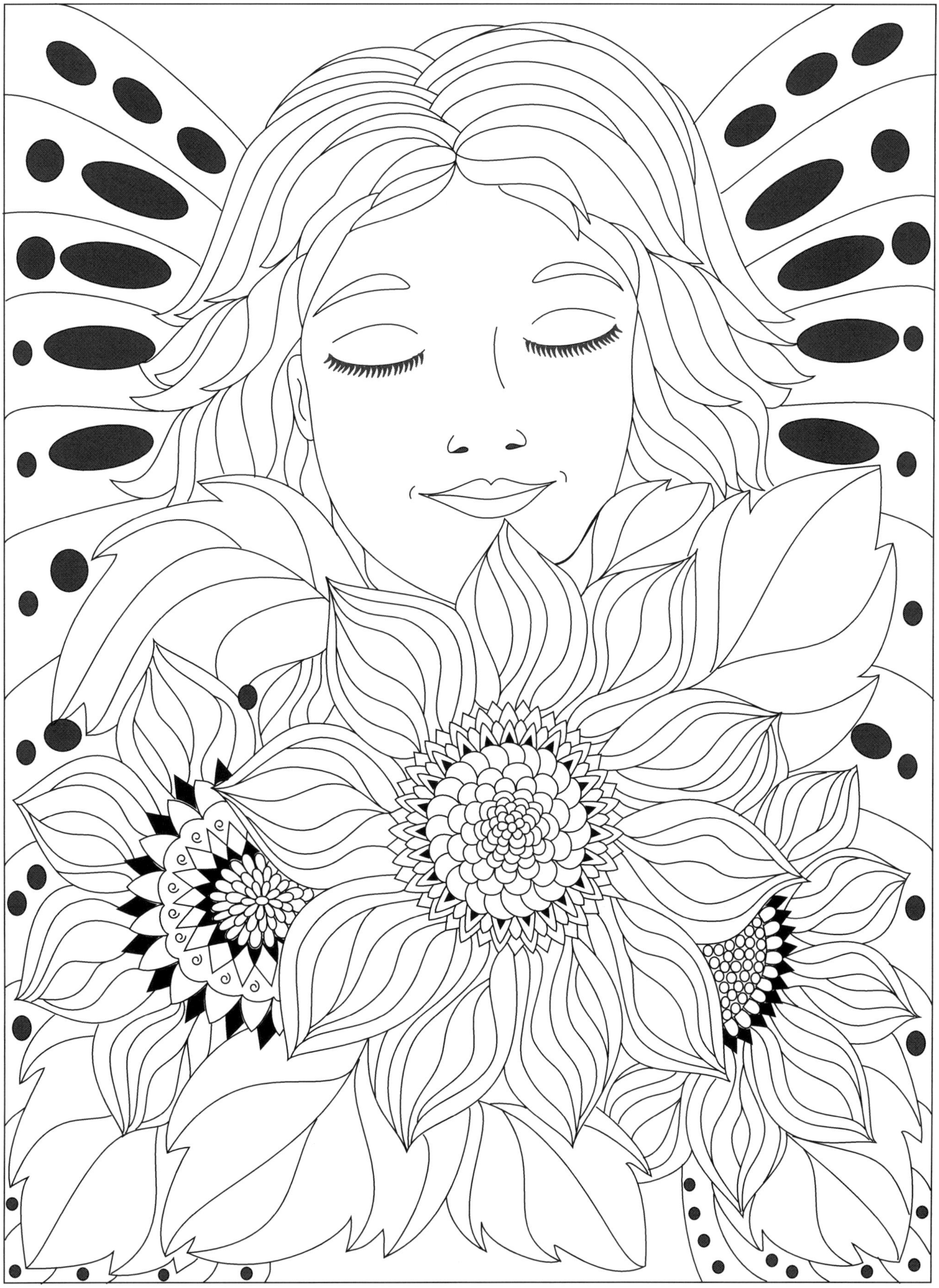

Never hide
your WINGS...

I AM PERFECT

JUST THE WAY I AM

My Strengths & Qualities

What I dream about:
_____
_____
_____

Things I am good at:
_____
_____
_____

What I like about my appearance:
_____
_____
_____

What makes me unique:
_____
_____
_____

Challenges I have overcome:
_____
_____
_____

Compliments I have received:
_____
_____
_____

How I've made others happy:
_____
_____
_____

What I value the most:
_____
_____
_____

EXPRESSIONS ~ ALL ABOUT ME

I worry about _____

I dream about _____

I am proud of _____

I am interested in _____

I am afraid of _____

I am good at _____

I struggle with _____

I feel like _____

I never _____

_____ makes me angry.

_____ makes me sad.

_____ makes me laugh.

SELF ESTEEM JOURNAL

MONDAY
Something I did well today... _____
I am thankful for... _____
I was proud of ... _____

TUESDAY
A positive thing I witnessed... _____
I am grateful for... _____
Today I accomplished ... _____

WEDNESDAY
Today was interesting because... _____
Something I did for someone... _____
I am grateful for... _____

THURSDAY
Something I did well today... _____
I am thankful for... _____
I was proud of ... _____

FRIDAY
A positive thing I witnessed... _____
I am grateful for... _____
Today I accomplished... _____

SATURDAY
Today was interesting because... _____
Something I did for someone... _____
I am grateful for... _____

SUNDAY
Something I did well today... _____
I had a positive experience with... _____
I was proud of ... _____

SELF ESTEEM JOURNAL

MONDAY
Something I did well today... _____
I am thankful for... _____
I was proud of ... _____

TUESDAY
A positive thing I witnessed... _____
I am grateful for... _____
Today I accomplished ... _____

WEDNESDAY
Today was interesting because... _____
Something I did for someone... _____
I am grateful for... _____

THURSDAY
Something I did well today... _____
I am thankful for... _____
I was proud of ... _____

FRIDAY
A positive thing I witnessed... _____
I am grateful for... _____
Today I accomplished... _____

SATURDAY
Today was interesting because... _____
Something I did for someone... _____
I am grateful for... _____

SUNDAY
Something I did well today... _____
I had a positive experience with... _____
I was proud of ... _____

SELF ESTEEM JOURNAL

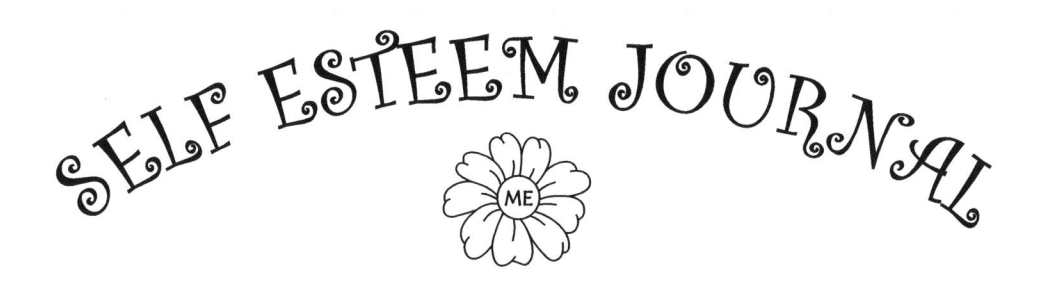

MONDAY
Something I did well today...
I am thankful for...
I was proud of...

TUESDAY
A positive thing I witnessed...
I am grateful for...
Today I accomplished...

WEDNESDAY
Today was interesting because...
Something I did for someone...
I am grateful for...

THURSDAY
Something I did well today...
I am thankful for...
I was proud of...

FRIDAY
A positive thing I witnessed...
I am grateful for...
Today I accomplished...

SATURDAY
Today was interesting because...
Something I did for someone...
I am grateful for...

SUNDAY
Something I did well today...
I had a positive experience with...
I was proud of...

SELF ESTEEM JOURNAL

MONDAY
Something I did well today...
I am thankful for...
I was proud of ...

TUESDAY
A positive thing I witnessed...
I am grateful for...
Today I accomplished ...

WEDNESDAY
Today was interesting because...
Something I did for someone...
I am grateful for...

THURSDAY
Something I did well today...
I am thankful for...
I was proud of ...

FRIDAY
A positive thing I witnessed...
I am grateful for...
Today I accomplished...

SATURDAY
Today was interesting because...
Something I did for someone...
I am grateful for...

SUNDAY
Something I did well today...
I had a positive experience with...
I was proud of ...

BUTTERFLY BEAUTIES

ALL ILLUSTRATIONS HAND DRAWN BY
JENNIFER E. ROBINSON

WWW.BUTTERFLYBEAUTIES.CO

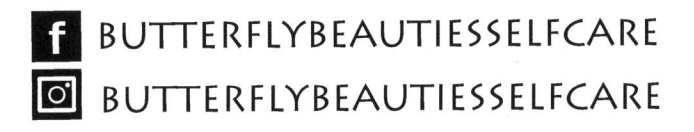

f BUTTERFLYBEAUTIESSELFCARE
◙ BUTTERFLYBEAUTIESSELFCARE

"DOWNLOAD YOUR FREE SELF-LOVE GUIDE
@ BUTTERFLYBEAUTIES.CO"

Jennifer Robinson is a self-taught artist living in the small town of Fergus, Ontario Canada. She loves meditation, nature and all creations of art. She is passionate about inspiring and empowering women and girls alike.

Drawing on her own past and sometimes painful experiences, her journals were created with the hopes that they would inspire, provide hope and remind you of your inner strength and beauty.

This Healing Journal is the first one in a series of 4 Self-Care Journals. The series will include 2 journals for women & 2 for teens/girls. For details on the other journals you can check the following:

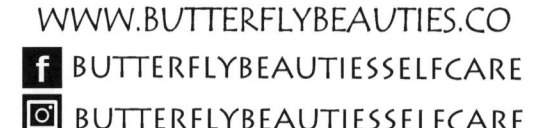

WWW.BUTTERFLYBEAUTIES.CO
BUTTERFLYBEAUTIESSELFCARE
BUTTERFLYBEAUTIESSELFCARE

In her journal series "Butterfly Beauties" she hopes to encourage and empower women and their daughters to find their true inner beauty as they colour, create and connect with their heart.

Made in the USA
Middletown, DE
12 June 2020